NEW MEXICO

A PICTURE MEMORY

CLB 2872
© 1993 Colour Library Books Ltd., Godalming, Surrey, England
All rights reserved
This 1993 edition published by Crescent Books,
distributed by Outlet Book Company, Inc., a Random House Company,
40 Engelhard Avenue, Avenel, New Jersey 07001
Color separations by Scantrans Pte Ltd., Singapore
Printed and bound in Singapore
ISBN 0 517 07261 0
8 7 6 5 4 3 2 1

Photography
Eduardo Fuss

Design
Teddy Hartshorn

Text
Bill Harris

Captions
Susan Hazen-Hammond
Nicola Dent

Editorial
David Gibbon

Production
Ruth Arthur
Sally Connolly
Neil Randles

Director of Production
Gerald Hughes

NEW MEXICO
A PICTURE MEMORY

CRESCENT BOOKS
NEW YORK · AVENEL, NEW JERSEY

Nearly everybody in America has heard about Billy the Kid. Authors from Zane Grey to Gore Vidal have written about him, and he has inspired songs by Bob Dylan and Billy Joel and a ballet score by Aaron Copeland. He was portrayed in the movies by Paul Newman and Roy Rogers, Lash LaRue and Robert Taylor, to name just a few, and articles about him have appeared in major magazines from the *Saturday Evening Post* to *Saturday Review*. But for all that, even among fans of the Wild West, naming the scene of the Kid's exploits is often as difficult as remembering Billy's last name.

Even though Audie Murphy's movie version of the story was called *The Kid From Texas*, everyone in New Mexico knew the truth, and almost all of the state south of Santa Fe and west of the Pecos River to the Mogollon Mountains is still called Billy the Kid Country. And even little kids living between Roswell and Silver City know that the outlaw answered to the name of William H. Bonney.

But Billy the Kid also often called himself Henry McCarty, and sometimes he said his real name was William Antrim. About all that is known for sure about him is that by the time he was fifteen he was a well-known juvenile delinquent in Silver City, and that he broke out of a jail there before appearing to answer charges of stealing clothes from a Chinese laundry. He spent the next couple of years working as a cowboy in Arizona and, when he was eighteen, the Kid escaped from jail a second time after a jury found him guilty of murdering a man in a barroom brawl. That led him back to New Mexico's Lincoln County, where he waded into the middle of a range war that was already attracting national attention.

On the surface, the feud was between cattle baron John Chisum and small ranchers over water and grazing rights. But the dispute was also between two political factions and conflicting banking interests. On one hand was the U.S. Attorney, who was also president of Santa Fe's only bank and the political boss of the Territory, and on the other side, Chisum and his companions, who longed to take control for themselves and started the ball rolling by opening a rival bank. When young Billy Bonney arrived, he got a job with one of Chisum's partners, John Tunstall, but the only fighting that was going on was on the financial front. Everything changed in 1878 when Tunstall lost his ranch after some shady legal manipulations, and when a posse arrived to claim his livestock, Billy and his fellow ranch hands sent them off empty-handed. A few days later, the same posse found Tunstall out on the range and shot him. When the Sheriff refused to arrest the killers, the citizens of Lincoln formed a posse of their own which they called "The Regulators," and one of its riders was Billy the Kid.

The Regulators had a quasi-legal status until they killed two of the men they were hunting, then they became hunted themselves. The Territorial Governor, a charter member of the so-called "Santa Fe Ring," revoked their status, and the posse became a target of both the sheriff's men and the army. With that, Billy the Kid was officially an outlaw; he was nineteen years old. Up to that point, he had been just another Regulator, but he made a name for himself when he ambushed and killed the local sheriff on the streets of Lincoln. Now the Kid had a price on his head – $200 dead or alive. In the meantime, open war had broken out and people didn't even go to church without their guns.

By mid-July, 1878, the whole town was under siege, and after a fierce gunfight, the Kid and a handful of former Regulators managed to make a heart-stopping escape from a burning house and set up new head-quarters at Fort Sumner. The street fighting had involved Federal troops, which was illegal, and when President Rutherford B. Hayes heard about it, he replaced the Governor with former Civil War General Lew Wallace, who offered amnesty to the Regulators and began to untangle the mess the range war had created.

Billy the Kid, meanwhile, was amusing himself rustling horses in Mexico, but he drifted back to Fort Sumner when he heard about the amnesty proclamation. It was a big mistake. Some of his friends had gone to work for James J. Dolan, once their sworn enemy, and the Kid thought he'd take advantage of the opportunity too. But when he met up with Dolan in a Lincoln saloon, the rancher had just shot a man and was in the process of soaking the body with whiskey so he could set fire to it. Knowing that, as a witness, his own days were numbered, the Kid later volunteered to go back to the saloon to put a gun in the corpse's hand to make the killing look like self-defense. But instead he headed for the hills again and, naturally, Dolan said he was the killer. Governor Wallace entered Billy's life at that point. He wanted the Kid's testimony in the killing, but he also wanted to know more about the recent range war, and he made a deal with Billy to give himself up. But when a jury found a gang of cattle rustlers innocent in spite of the Kid's testimony against them, he realized that the Governor didn't have the power to protect him, and he broke out of jail to became a cattle rustler himself. His chief target was his former employer, John Chisum.

A fugitive again, the Kid played a cat and mouse game with posses sent out to find him, and continued stealing cattle and defending his reputation as the handiest man with a gun in the whole Territory. During this time, he made a formidable enemy of a former friend, Pat Garrett, the newly-elected Sheriff of Lincoln County. Garrett finally caught up with him at Sinking Springs and took him into custody. He was found guilty of the murder of the former sheriff and sentenced to hang, but two weeks before the scheduled execution the Kid escaped, killing two of his guards in the process, and rode off with shackles still fastened to his wrists.

He should have headed for the border, of course, but instead he holed up at a nearby ranch where Garrett found him three months later, and one shot to the chest was all it took to end the career of Billy the Kid. He was not quite twenty-two years old. He had actually killed four men and was part of gangs that dispatched five others, but he was famous from coast to coast as a cold-blooded killer, and obituary writers as far away as London claimed he had killed a man for each year of his life, somewhat like snuffing out birthday candles. And a Santa Fe newspaper reported, in all seriousness, that when the Kid fell dead, "a dark figure with wings of a dragon, claws like a tiger, eyes like balls of fire, and horns like a bison" was seen hovering over the corpse. There is no question that Billy the Kid was not a good boy, but his problem seems to have been that he made the wrong kinds of enemies among bankers, sheriffs and cattle barons. His only friend in a high place was Lew Wallace, the Territorial Governor. But, if Wallace wanted to help, his hands were tied and he had other more important things on his mind; during his tenure in Santa Fe, the former general was busy writing a novel called Ben Hur.

With that accomplishment, Lew Wallace might qualify as New Mexico's first artist-in-residence, a tradition that continues to this day. It actually began centuries before him with the work of native cultures, whose buildings and artifacts have yet to be equaled, but artists began arriving in New Mexico in the 1890s, willing to give it a try. The first of them was Joseph H. Sharp, who fell in love with the landscape and the quality of the light in Taos and went back East to spread the word. Artists who followed him didn't see any point in leaving, and Taos soon became an influential art colony.

Its influence became international in 1916, when Mabel Dodge arrived and fell in love, not only with Taos, but with a local Indian whom she married. It was the same Mabel Dodge who had moved to Paris as a young woman, swearing never to have anything to do with America again. A rich heiress, she established a salon to encourage Parisian artists, and settled down to keep her vow. But when her young son reached school age, she decided that the only place he could get a decent education was in the United States, and she moved to New York's Greenwich Village. Her transplanted salon turned the Village into a mecca for artists and writers and, by moving on to Taos, she had the same influence on New Mexico, luring such friends as D.H. Lawrence, Aldous Huxley and Willa Cather to share her discovery. Before long there were other important art colonies in Albuquerque and Santa Fe, and what may be the most significant contribution to the New Mexico art scene came in the person of Georgia O'Keeffe, one of the greatest painters in American history, during the late 1920s.

The twentieth-century painters gave a new meaning to the native arts and, thanks to them, Indian pottery and blankets, silver work and sculpture finally became recognized as important and valuable creations. It was about time. The Mogollon culture that thrived in Southwestern New Mexico as far back as 300 B.C. is considered the most advanced of all the early Southwestern tribes, and its red and brown ceramics were centuries ahead of their time. When the tribe vanished, the Anasazi who followed were not only accomplished pottery designers, but also constructed highly-advanced pueblos and, even though horses and the wheel were unknown to them, they constructed a network of roads that would have been the envy of the Romans.

Creativity had to take a back seat to survival after the Spanish came in search of gold in the 1530s. They came and went for almost 300 years, and by the end of the eighteenth century there were only nineteen of the original eighty pueblos still functioning, and four of them had been relocated to different, safer sites. But by then the Conquistadors and the Native Americans had learned to live together, and the settlements along the Rio Grande in present-day New Mexico formed the most peaceful corner of all the Spanish territory in the New World.

They were far enough away from Mexico City and the influence of the Viceroy and his minions to be as independent as the Anglo colonies along the Eastern seaboard. And they were far enough from the new United States to ensure that neither group was even aware that the other existed. That state of affairs changed one day in 1806, when an expedition led by General Zebulon Pike appeared on the horizon. It had been sent out to explore the Rocky Mountain territory that had been included in the Louisiana Purchase, and either by accident or design wandered south into New Spain.

Pike wasn't exactly given a warm welcome. He was arrested and moved to Santa Fe, where his maps and notes were taken away, and then he and his men were unceremoniously escorted back to the Mississippi and released with a warning to stay on their own side of the river. But in spite of the treatment he received, Pike was clearly impressed by the Southwest. He subsequently wrote a book about his adventures and his descriptions of the potential of the Santa Fe area convinced hundreds to follow in his footsteps. But the Spanish gave most of them the same treatment they had given Pike, and it wasn't until 1821, when Mexico became independent of Spain, that traders were able to blaze a trail to Santa Fe. They went by the thousands over the newly created Santa Fe Trail, and in a matter of months, along with trappers moving south from the Rockies, the Americans were firmly in charge, even though the territory was still a part of Mexico and would be for another twenty-five years.

During the Mexican War, General Stephen Kearny led his army into Santa Fe and managed to take the whole territory without firing a shot. Except for a bloody, but unsuccessful, revolt among the Spanish settlers in Taos after Kearny had moved on, New Mexico had become an American possession. The 1848 treaty that ended the war added California and New Mexico, which at the time included what is now Arizona, to the map of the United States. Two years later, after settling a nasty border dispute with Texas, New Mexico was officially declared a U.S. Territory, but another sixty-two years went by before it became the forty-seventh state in 1912.

During those years, the Apache and Navajo Indians were fighting for their own rights, but it was a losing battle. The Navajo were driven from their ancestral lands and their farms were burned behind them. Faced with what was clearly a no-win situation, they finally agreed to the Government's offer of worthless land along the Pecos River and were force-marched across New Mexico to take up life on the reservation. The Mescalero Apache, who shared the land with them, finally moved on and went back to their old ways, but the Navajo stayed where they were for close to seven years of near-starvation before the Government decided to do something about them. As inhospitable as the reservation was, the land of the Navajos' ancestors in Northwestern New Mexico seemed, to the white man at least, even more hostile. But, ironically, when given a choice, they picked the country "our God created for us," and they are still there. The Apache tribes were relocated to the northern part of the Territory, too. All of them, that is, except the Chiricahua, who held out for nearly twenty more years under such legendary leaders as Geronimo and Victorio. By the time New Mexico became a state there were less than 200 Chiricahua left and, on their promise to behave, they were allowed to resettle in their former homeland.

The end of the Indian threat brought the cattle kings in from Texas, and discoveries of gold and silver brought prospectors from all over the United States. In 1881, when the Southern Pacific Railroad met the Atchison, Topeka & Santa Fe, New Mexico became an important crossroads of a transcontinental railroad and the boom was on. Like every other boom in every other part of the country, the real treasure was the land itself, and lawyers and real estate speculators managed to get rich buying and selling millions of acres. In their frenzy they even found ways to sell land to the children of Spanish farmers, who had inherited the same acreage from their fathers.

Farming had always been a chancy business in New Mexico, and in the 1930s a long drought put most of the state's small farmers out of business, and sent the real estate men looking for greener pastures when New Mexico's land values fell to the lowest on the continent. It began to look as though the state's future was going to be tied to tourism alone, but a new industry was coming that not even the most imaginative could have predicted.

In the early days of World War II, physicist J. Robert Oppenheimer was given the job of finding a location for a base to develop an atomic bomb. He had spent his boyhood summers in Northern New Mexico and remembered a remote school in the mountains near Santa Fe, at a place called Los Alamos. It was a perfect place, he said, and in 1942 the school was surrounded by a small city of scientists, military people and their families living in complete isolation and total secrecy.

On July 16, 1945, at 5:30 in the morning, the first atomic bomb was detonated at a remote site in the New Mexico badlands, and the world hasn't been the same since. The flash of light was seen hundreds of miles away, and its mushroom cloud rose seven miles into the air. It was the most destructive force ever created by man, but at the same time it gave New Mexico a kind of new lease on life. No place on earth has made more contributions to finding applications for nuclear energy, and such institutions as the Los Alamos and Sandia Laboratories have provided jobs and a reason to relocate in New Mexico, for thousands.

But most of the people who visit Los Alamos don't go there to see the birthplace of the atomic bomb. There are much better, much older, reasons. The city's boosters have counted no less than 7,000 sites important to Native American cultures, including seven pueblos in the area, and nearby Espanola, the earliest Spanish settlement in the state, has kept the Hispanic culture vividly alive. Not far from there is Abiquiu, where Georgia O'Keeffe lived and was inspired for many years, all just a stone's throw from the edge of Billy the Kid Country and Santa Fe.

But North-Central New Mexico isn't the only part of the state where three distinct cultures exist side by side. The people who gave it the name "The Land of Enchantment" had gorgeous landscapes in mind, and no one could possibly disagree that it is an enchantingly beautiful place. But a big part of the enchantment of New Mexico is the way Native Americans, Hispanics and Anglos have learned to live together, in spite of a long history of hostility, without giving up their own traditions. And it is the mix of traditions that makes New Mexico unique among the fifty states.

Volcanic Shiprock (facing page top), considered sacred by the Navajo Indians, towers above the surrounding landscape. Facing page bottom and below: Bisti Wilderness, with its stark landscape of sculpted sandstone pillars, and (overleaf) an atmospheric sunset near Farmington.

Facing page: one of North America's major archaeological sites, Chaco Culture National Historical Park features numerous Anasazi Indian ruins that include magnificent Pueblo Bonito (top) and Chetro Ketl (bottom). Below: Aztec Ruins National Monument, also a former Anasazi settlement.

Once a prosperous boom town, abandoned Elizabethtown (above left) is just one of the sites in northern New Mexico that boasts a gold-mining or Wild West past. Other historic attractions in the area include a fine collection of Western memorabilia at Springer (below left), the Cumbres & Toltec Scenic Railroad at Chama (left), and the 1872 St. James Hotel (below), still in use at Cimarron. Facing page: overviews of Red River (top) and Raton (bottom). Above: the village of Questa, particularly noted for its excellent honey, and (overleaf) colorful cottonwoods brighten the somber walls of Cimarron Canyon.

In the early 1600s the Spanish established a mission at Taos, and today many fine Catholic churches, including Our Lady of Sorrows (above), reflect these origins. In the 1800s the town became an important center for the fur trade, and the Kit Carson Home and Museum (below) celebrates the most famed of the visiting mountainmen, who married into a local Taos family. During the 1900s Taos developed into an important arts community, and today features both galleries (above right) and the homes of noted artists such as Leon Gaspard (right). Facing page: Taos Pueblo, the oldest and most picturesque of the state's nineteen Indian villages.

Ranchos de Taos, near Taos, is renowned for the impressive San Francisco de Asís (below), thought to be the most photographed church in the nation. Facing page: Taos Pueblo, with the ruins of the old mission church (top) destroyed in the 1847 Revolt, and its newer, San Geronimo (bottom).

23

The beautiful High Road to Taos, or Camino Alto, winds through the foothills of the Sangre de Cristo Mountains (bottom right), forming a link between Santa Fe and Taos. Below: the Santa Cruz Reservoir, located between Chimayo and Cundiyo – two of the Spanish-speaking villages in this mountainous region. Right and center right: dramatic Rio Grande Gorge State Park, named for the river that has carved this remarkable canyon, and (overleaf) the serene waters of Abiquiu Lake.

The Harvest (below left), Comanche (left and below), and Corn (above left) dances are among the elaborate and colorful celebrations that are so much a part of the Anasazi Indian culture. Certain communities also celebrate their own specific feast days such as San Ildefonso's Day – during which villagers perform the Animal Dance (facing page top) – and Santa Clara's Day (above). Facing page bottom: the village church at San Ildefonso.

30

Below and center right: the dramatic adobe ruins of 19th-century Fort Union, once the major military post in the Southwest, and now preserved as a striking national monument. To the south is Las Vegas, founded in 1835, and featuring a number of historic adobe buildings in the Old Town Plaza and downtown area (right), many constructed before the introduction of the railway. Bottom right: the distinctive ruin, of a once-extensive pueblo, in Pecos National Historical Park.

The area surrounding Santa Fe is one of great variety and color, with the gray of Tent Rocks (facing page top), near Cochiti Lake, contrasting with the gold of wildflowers below the Ortiz Mountains (facing page bottom) and of aspens (below) within the Sangre de Cristo Mountains.

Glorieta Battlefield, near Pecos, is the site of an important Civil War battle in which Confederate troops were forced to retreat from the state. Today, soldiers dressed in traditional blue and gray uniforms (facing page, above and right) reenact the fighting that took place in 1862. A little to the southwest of Glorieta are the towns of Galisteo (below) and its neighbor Madrid (above right), a former coal mining community, which boasts the Old Coal Mine Museum (below right) as its main attraction.

Once the site of an Indian pueblo, Santa Fe (these pages) is the oldest capital and seat of government in the United States. Among the cultural attractions of this ancient city are the Museum of Fine Arts (below left), the Fletcher Gallery and the Phil Daves Studio/Gallery that it faces (left), and the open-air Santa Fe Opera House (above left). Also of interest is the variety of architectural styles to be found in the city center, especially along East San Francisco Street (facing page), with the impressive Romanesque-style Cathedral of St. Francis of Assisi (below) nearby. Above: a historic structure in a suburb museum. Overleaf: the popular Santa Fe Ski Basin, which lies above the capital amid the Sangre de Cristo Mountains.

Santa Fe's many annual festivities reflect something of its blend of Indian and Spanish cultures. Below left and facing page top: the Fiesta de Santa Fe, often considered "the oldest ongoing community celebration in the nation," commemorates the return of the Spanish after the 1680 Pueblo Revolt, and (below) a related religious parade. Other annual events include the selling of Indian arts and crafts at the Mountain Man Trade Fair and Buffalo Roast (above left) and at Indian Market (facing page bottom). Each spring and fall costumed volunteers reenact the past (left and above) at the suburb museum of El Rancho de las Golondrinas. Overleaf: the railroad station at Santa Fe.

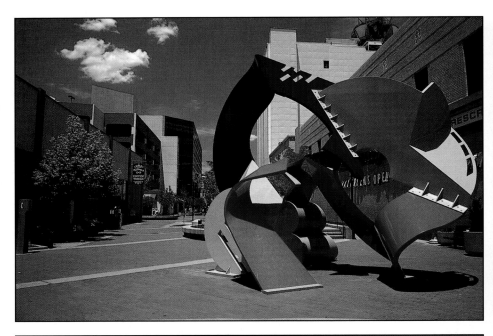

Straddling the mighty Rio Grande at the geographic center of the state, Albuquerque (these pages) is New Mexico's largest city. The original 1708 settlement is preserved within the Old Town, with the impressive San Felipe de Neri Church (below) as its focal point. In contrast is downtown Albuquerque, which features the Civic Plaza (below left) and a brightly colored abstract sculpture (above left) among its attractions. Left: the New Mexico Museum of Natural History, to the north of the city, and (above and facing page) the spectacular and colorful Albuquerque Balloon Fiesta, said to be one of the most heavily photographed events in the United States.

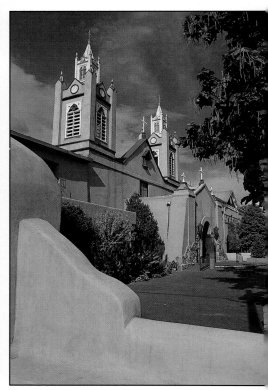

Left: the distinctive profile of the Ladron Mountains and (center left) the broad expanse of the Rio Grande River, edged with fall-colored cottonwoods, are both features of the area south of Belen. Also in the vicinity are the gray, limestone ruins of Gran Quivira (bottom left) and the red walls of Quarai (below), two of the three Indian pueblos preserved within Salinas Pueblo Missions National Monument. Overleaf: a stunning view of the Bosque del Apache wildlife refuge.

Crowned by the stunning underground scenery of Carlsbad Caverns National Park (facing page top and above), New Mexico is a state of strange and varied natural splendor. Hardened lava and contorted rocks in the Valley of Fire State Park (below), and the gypsum dunefield at White Sands National Monument (facing page bottom) illustrate this diversity. Above right: brilliant green and red chiles at the village of Hatch, and (overleaf) extensive chile fields around Las Cruces. Right: White City's Apache Canyon Trading Post, and (below right) the Space Hall of Fame at Alamogordo.

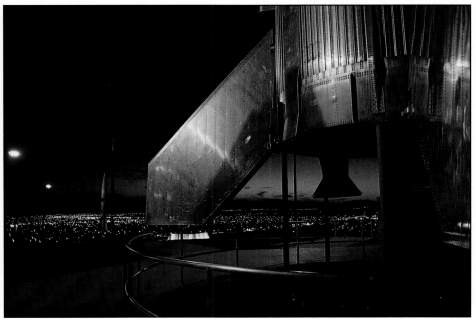

Among New Mexico's twenty-nine state parks are City of Rocks (below), with its fine sculpted forms, and Rock Hound (facing page bottom), noted for its exotic stones. Facing page top and overleaf: the Organ Mountains overlooking Las Cruces. Last page: wildflowers and prickly pear cacti.